Original title:
Frozen Mornings, Shattered Nights

Copyright © 2024 Creative Arts Management OÜ
All rights reserved.

Author: Zachary Prescott
ISBN HARDBACK: 978-9916-94-516-2
ISBN PAPERBACK: 978-9916-94-517-9

Glacial Secrets Beneath the Stars

In the chill, my nose turned red,
I stumbled on ice, fell on my head.
The stars above did laugh with glee,
As I skated around like a giddy bee.

A penguin squad witnessed my plight,
They waddled and cheered under the night.
I grinned at my blunder, brushed off the snow,
Who knew I'd become a frozen show?

Remnants of Radiance in the Frost

Morning's glow with a hint of fun,
I found a snowman just for a pun.
He had a carrot for a nose so bright,
"Want to build more? Let's catch some light!"

But Mr. Snowman just wouldn't chat,
He melted the moment I grabbed my hat.
Though he faded, his smile stayed,
In frosty laughter, our fun replayed.

A Dance of Light and Shadows

At dawn, the sun began to peek,
My shadow did a little cheeky streak.
It danced around, gave me a fright,
Challenged me to a waltz in the light.

"Let's tango!" I said, with a merry grin,
But my shadow tripped, fell right in.
It rolled in the snow, then waved its hands,
In this winter's ball, we made our plans.

Nectar of Silence in the Chill

The air was crisp; I took a sip,
Of hot cocoa on a frosty trip.
But a snowflake fell right in my mug,
It swirled and danced, a chilly thug.

So I shouted, "Hey, don't be rude!"
The marshmallows giggled; they were in the mood.
With laughter, we toasted to the frosty spree,
In winter's embrace, we drank with glee.

Crystals in the Remnants of Night

Jellybeans glimmer on my lawn,
A candy-coated dusk is drawn.
The stars above begin to giggle,
While snowmen do a little wiggle.

Squirrels in scarves chase after trails,
Searching for nuts like silly tales.
A frozen dance upon the grass,
With mocktails made of frosty sass.

Lament of the Shattered Moonlight

The moon got stuck in a pie tin,
Yelling for help, it can't begin.
A flash of light, a brilliant fall,
The stars all cheer, then trip and sprawl.

An owl winks at the sun's first beam,
As sleepy clouds start forming steam.
The shadows laugh, they cannot hide,
In a night gone absolutely wide.

A Shimmering Veil Before Daybreak

Glitter spills from twilight's pouch,
Covering my neighbor's couch.
The cat wears boots and tries to skate,
Slipping around with such great fate.

While coffee brews in giddy peaks,
The rooster crows; it starts to speak.
A laughter fills the chilly air,
As dreams are caught in frosty snares.

Twilight's Grasp on a Sleeping World

The world is wrapped in blankets tight,
While gnomes hold disco balls at night.
They dance and prance with frozen toes,
In shadows where the humor flows.

A dandelion dreams of snow,
Saying, "Just chill! You'll never know!"
As laughter twinkles in the cold,
A symphony of warmth unfolds.

Lullabies of a Shattered Twilight

In the cold of night, my socks can't find,
They vanished somewhere, left me in a bind.
I search in the drawer, a laugh on my face,
Who knew my feet could enter a sock race?

A cat sneezes softly, gives me a scare,
I jump in my chair, pretend I don't care.
The bits of the moon, all covered in frost,
Yet here I sit, with a tea that's been lost.

Memory's Chill in the Dawn

The toast pops up with a comical jump,
Butter flies off in a humorous thump.
My coffee spills like the rain on parade,
Hey, breakfast brawls! Who needs a charade?

I grab my scarf, but it's stuck in the chair,
What looks like a fashion just doesn't compare.
The laughter it brings warms the frost in my toes,
And giggles abound as the chaos just grows.

Chilled Echoes of the Nightfall

The stars twinkle bright, a wild, wacky dance,
I trip on my slippers; not quite my last chance.
The moon winks at me, like it's heard this before,
As I tumble and giggle across the ice floor.

A snowman is built, but it looks more like me,
With buttons for eyes and a hat oh-so-free.
I laugh 'til I cry at this lumpy delight,
He's my frosty buddy on this peculiar night.

Glistening Shadows of Forgotten Paths

In the crisp morning air, I hear a loud crunch,
Turns out it's my cereal, oh what a punch!
The flakes fly about, a bright, silly mess,
Breakfast ballet? I'll surely confess.

The snow piles high, but I can't find my car,
It's hiding quite well, like a lost candy bar.
With a giggle I wander, all lost in a game,
Who knew morning chores could be so full of fame?

The Twilight of a Shivering Heart

The sun peeked out, oh what a tease,
My morning coffee's gone cold with ease.
I slipped on ice, did a little dance,
The neighbor's cat gave me a glance.

My breath is steam, I'm wearing socks,
I thought it was warm, but lost my box.
The dog just laughed, he's full of pride,
As I leap like a goat in a frantic stride.

Snowflakes fall, and I try to catch,
A wild snowball hits my poor old hatch.
The kids are giggling, oh what a sight,
While I faceplant, in pure delight.

The twilight glows, my cheeks are red,
I'll drink hot cocoa, or go back to bed.
But every slip, every laugh, and cheer,
Makes winter nights a bit less severe.

Icebound Memories in a Timeworn Abyss

Chilly winds whisper tales of frost,
My memories melt, but they're not lost.
An icicle hangs, like a pointed hat,
I dodge it quickly, that's where I'm at!

A penguin waltzes, or is it my mind?
The snowman sighs, he's been in a bind.
Hot chocolate's ready, with whipped cream art,
I sip and reflect on my shivering heart.

Laughter echoes from windows aglow,
I once built a fort, but it was a no-show.
With my shovel in hand, I made a grand scene,
A castle of snow turned soft and mean.

Now the night falls, my plans in a bunch,
Staring at the fridge—oh, what a lunch!
But in this abyss, where stories collide,
I find my joy, with laughter as my guide.

Beneath the Glimmering Ice Tapestry

Icicles hang like crystal charms,
A snowman with big, silly arms.
Frosty hair in a winter haze,
He smiles wide, despite the freeze phase.

Penguins dance on frozen lakes,
Waddle along, oh what a quake!
With snowballs tossed and laughter loud,
They slide and spin, a feathery crowd.

Shadows Quiver in the Awakening

Night brings a chill, but what a sight,
A squirrel in pajamas, now that's a fright!
Under the moon, they do a jig,
Chasing their tails—oh, look at him dig!

With twinkling lights, the world's aglow,
Jack Frost's prank, and watch the show.
Neighbors slip on a patch of ice,
Laughter erupts—oh, isn't that nice?

Hushed Echoes of a Bitter Winter

An old cat snuggles, her warmth in tow,
With a steaming cup, I sip so slow.
Snowflakes tumble like soft little hats,
On top of my nose, oh where are the cats?

The wind howls jokes through hollow trees,
While flurries play tag and skip with ease.
Chirping birds, they shiver and strut,
Finding their rhythm—oh, wait, what's that?

Glimpses of Life Beneath the Ice

Under the chill, the world asleep,
A raccoon in a dumpster, oh he takes a leap!
With a laugh and a dance, he stirs up the trash,
While frozen cheeks turn a rosy splash.

Each dawn reveals a frosty scene,
Where frostbite's laughter fills the screen.
The sun peeks in, it's a brand new day,
And all the snowmen are on their way.

Echoes of a Chilled Dawn

When the sun forgets to wake up tight,
And even the coffee's bundled up right.
Socks mismatched in a frosty dance,
I trip on ice, oh, what a chance!

The cat's on the rug, judging my plight,
While I'm sipped on air, my breath's a misty sight.
Snowflakes tumble, giggling like fools,
Whispering secrets to my frozen shoes.

Rime-Kissed Reveries

The air is crisp, my nose's a berry,
Why is my hair so wild and hairy?
With mittens that laugh at my silly chase,
I dance with the frost, a curious embrace.

Hot cocoa's a stranger, it stares at me,
"What's with your hat? It's a fashion catastrophe!"
The marshmallows bounce, they're in on the jest,
Like mini snowmen in a sticky quest.

Silhouettes in the Frost

In early hours, the squirrels plot,
While I'm still dreaming of breakfast hot.
A snowman winks as I pass on by,
Is he critiquing my scarf? Oh my, oh my!

Frosted windows, a picture frame,
I squint and wonder, are all pets the same?
The dog is wrapped in his bulky coat,
He's living the life, a furry remote.

Midnight's Crystal Veil

Stars twinkle like they're in a play,
While curtains of ice freeze the day.
I'll catch a comet and ride it high,
Just me and my dreams, oh, my oh my!

Gloves with holes, what a silly sight,
Fingers poke out, and it feels just right.
A snowball fight with shadows I make,
Who knew that winter could cause such a shake?

The Shard of Light That Breaks the Dark

The sun peeks in, with a grin so wide,
Its rays like arrows, we can't quite hide.
Socks gone missing, where did they flee?
A dance of shadows on toast and tea.

With laughter shared, we trip and fall,
The cat thinks he's king, he rules us all.
But in this play, we find delight,
As morning breaks, and chases the night.

Glistening Veils Over a Wistful Earth

A blanket of white, the world asleep,
We build a snowman, his secrets we keep.
With carrots for noses, and buttons anew,
He gives a wink as we frolic through.

The trees wear hats, oh what a sight,
And squirrels are plotting a snowball fight.
Giggles erupt with each chilly shove,
In this glistening game, we find our love.

Waking Beneath a Crystal Skies

Awake with a yawn, and a twist of fate,
Coffee spills over, oh is it too late?
The sky is aglow, like a firefly's dance,
A world full of giggles, a whimsical chance.

Pajamas askew, we wave our cheer,
As we shove aside worries, hold them dear.
In this crystal chill, joy freely flows,
We chase after dreams, where laughter grows.

Luminescence in the Depths of Winter

Stars twinkle brightly, like candy on trees,
We gather the warmth, wrapped snug as can be.
With cocoa in hand, and marshmallows galore,
Laughter erupts as we slide on the floor.

Snowflakes like confetti, a winter parade,
With a sprinkle of magic, our worries delayed.
Join in the fun with a delightful shout,
Even in cold, this warmth's never out.

The Haunting of a Frostbitten Heart

In the middle of frost, I lost my remote,
The TV won't play, it's stuck with a note.
The ghosts of my snacks haunt the pantry door,
They laughed as they crunched on the popcorn floor.

My heart took a chill, wrapped tight with some lace,
But who needs a heart when you've got a great space?
The chill in the air made me dance with my socks,
Turns out my new moves just confuse all the clocks.

Frosted Dreams in Dusk's Embrace

With curtains of ice and a warm cup in hand,
I dreamt of a beach, with soft golden sand.
But then I woke up to the snow's frosty bite,
Where my dreams melted fast, like chocolate at night.

The cats in their coats look like marshmallow fluff,
While I search for my gloves, did I buy them or bluff?
The snowman I built now demands to be fed,
With a carrot for lunch and some pie for his head.

The Chime of Icy Echoes

Bells jingle like magic, but they're frozen in time,
As I slip on the porch, it's a slapstick mime.
Icicles dangle like teeth from the roof,
As I dodge and I weave, searching for some proof.

Echoes of laughter bounce off the white walls,
As I chase my lost hat that rolls like a ball.
It flips and it flops, in a dance with the breeze,
While I tumble and twirl, laughing hard at my knees.

When Time Stopped in Silver Stillness

At dawn, I found breakfast all solid and cold,
The cereal froze like it was paid in gold.
The clock on the wall just gave up and froze,
While I snuck some cash from the bank of my nose.

In winter's embrace, the slippers escape,
A dance in the hall, oh what a great shape!
With socks left behind like troublesome ghosts,
I tumble through time with my breakfast-time boasts.

A Veil of White Over Broken Whispers

A snowman stands, with a hat awry,
Waving to birds with a curious eye.
His nose's a carrot, but quite a scam,
The squirrels just snicker, 'What a ham!'

Frosty flakes dance, and children scream,
As snowball fights become the dream.
But one fell throw, and oh what laughter,
They slip and slide, then chase thereafter!

Shrouded in the Hush of Winter

The world outside wears a chilly coat,
While mugs of cocoa make us gloat.
But watch out for cats, they're on the prowl,
Stealing snowflakes with a sly growl!

In quiet corners, penguins slide,
On ice-skates made from a shoelace bribe.
A waltz to remember in the snowy light,
As winter dreams dance in the silent night.

Ethereal Glimpse at Daybreak

At dawn's first glow, the world awakes,
With coffee spills and pan-to-make shakes.
A gleam on ice like gems in a chest,
But first comes the tumble, a comical quest!

Cats on the windowsill bask in sun,
While we chase our socks—oh, what fun!
They plot and plan from a snug little nook,
While we fumble about, just trying to cook.

Heartbeats Beneath a Layer of Ice

Underneath the chill, the heart beats loud,
But frozen toes make us laugh out proud.
With every treacherous step we take,
A slip and a slide, for goodness' sake!

Eager snowflakes fall, making patches to play,
While snow forts rise, come what may.
A glorious battle of snow and cold,
But watch for the icicle, tales to be told!

Chasing Echoes in the Morning Light

On a frosty field, I ran too fast,
Tripped on my laces, what a blast!
The sun peeked out, giving a grin,
And laughed at my fall, where to begin?

Hot cocoa spills, I claim it's art,
Marshmallows floating, a winter's heart.
Sipping slowly, the warmth I chase,
As a squirrel cheers me on—what a race!

Thorns of Night Beneath the Ice

Under the stars, my feet were cold,
With slippers that glimmered, I felt quite bold!
A chill comes creeping, what a fright,
But my furry hat said, 'You'll be alright!'

The dog chased shadows, barking in jest,
While I made snow angels, what a quest!
Out in the dark, a snowball planned,
Instead hit a tree—oh, how it spanned!

Radiant Whispers in a Shattered Realm

In the dead of night, I tried to sing,
A serenade to the moon, such a thing!
But my voice froze up, it gave a crack,
The stars all giggled, not holding back!

With a snowman's hat and a carrot nose,
I danced around him, striking poses.
He didn't clap, but I could swear,
His button eyes sparkled with a flair!

Kaleidoscope of Frost on the Ground

Crystal patterns twinkling nice,
I stomped them flat, now isn't that ice?
Each crunch was music, a symphonic beat,
As I pranced around, oh what a feat!

The ground was a canvas, my feet the brush,
Creating a masterpiece, in a joyful rush.
But then I slipped and did a twirl,
Making snowflakes laugh, oh what a whirl!

The Edge of Day in Silver and Blue

With pillow forts and breakfast fights,
We laugh through chilly, sleepy nights.
The coffee pot's a grumpy queen,
Its royal brew is fit for dreams.

Mittens lost in fluff and grace,
We build a snowman with a face.
He winks at us, then tips his hat,
While pigeons plot to steal my cat.

The sunlight creeps, a golden thief,
We chase our shadows, brief belief.
In shimmers bright, we dance around,
While icy laughter is the sound.

So as the day begins to glow,
We'll ride the waves of winter's flow.
With warm socks on and hearts so wide,
We'll greet the world with a giddy stride.

Tread Softly on the Ice of Dreams

Our dreams are skates on frozen streams,
We twirl and spin, or so it seems.
But watch your step, don't lose your grace,
You might just land on winter's face.

A penguin lends a helping flipper,
With every slip, we giggle quicker.
The ice might crack, but don't you fret,
For all good friends we won't regret.

There's cocoa here with marshmallow boats,
As we sail on the laughter floats.
So grab a friend and lend a cheer,
We'll conquer dreams without a fear.

Through icy paths we dance and slide,
On dreams we glide with arms open wide.
Each frosty laugh, a spark ignites,
As we embrace the dazzling nights.

Silent Frost on the Windowpane

The patterns bloom like winter's cheer,
On glass they swirl, our giggles near.
A snowflake sneeze, a chilly blast,
We write our names, but not too fast.

In secret whispers, snowflakes fall,
They tickle noses, one and all.
A snowball fight breaks out in glee,
With laughter echoing like the sea.

The cat outside is on a quest,
To catch the flakes — what a jest!
And as he pounces with a twist,
We toast to mornings, cooing bliss.

The world is wrapped, a frosty treat,
With cozy hats and warm, soft feet.
We sip our cocoa, hands entwined,
In winter's chill, we warm our minds.

Echoes of Dawn's Embrace

The rooster crows, he's had his fun,
The sun peeks out, a sleepy one.
We bundle up, not quite awake,
While dreaming still of frosty bake.

The dog has found a snowy throne,
He sits and guards his happy bone.
With frosty breath and floppy ears,
He howls for fun, and so, no fears.

With snowflakes in my cereal bowl,
I mix my milk for morning's role.
The fridge is filled with dreams unmet,
But breakfast sings, we won't forget.

So here we sit, with laughter bright,
Embracing all that's frosty light.
With echoes dancing in our hearts,
We greet the dawn, where magic starts.

Veil of Ice on the Silent Landscape

The snowflakes dance like lost ballet,
They trip and stumble in their play.
A snowman sneezes, what a sight,
His carrot nose took off in flight.

Socks on feet, oh what a scene,
Slipping and sliding like a marine.
The dog barks back at the icy air,
While neighbors gawk at his frosty flair.

A snowplow rumbles, grumbling loud,
Clearing the way through the fluffy crowd.
But oh! A snowball flies with glee,
Hits the driver—now that's funny!

Twilight descends, the skies are gray,
The moon peeks out, joins the play.
How ironic is the frosty fun,
With laughter echoing, we have won!

Fragments of Dreams in the Chill

Beneath a quilt of white so thick,
Dreams of summer, oh so slick.
But ice cream cones turn to icy blocks,
When the sun falls victim to winter's shocks.

Mittens shriek at a bold snowball,
A penguin wobbles, laughing for all.
The icicles hang like sparkling teeth,
Joking about their lack of warmth beneath.

The cat hides tight in the sweater's fold,
While mice wear coats, brave and bold.
They scamper around, causing a mess,
As winter giggles at their cold duress.

In the distance, a hot cocoa's song,
With marshmallow dreams where hearts belong.
The laughter flows, oh what a thrill,
We share our glee beneath the chill!

Whispers of an Unyielding Dawn

The rooster crows, but what a fright,
His comb turned blue in the morning light.
He slips on ice and twirls about,
Then fluffs his feathers with a shout.

Sledding kids zoom by with flair,
While nearby snowmen collect their hair.
With carrot sticks thrown in for fun,
They plot and plan their snowman run.

The frostbite nibbles on toes so cold,
Yet laughter warms the hearts so bold.
As breakfast brews, one must concede,
To humor's touch—we're finally freed.

The sun peeks through the icy haze,
Warming hearts with rays ablaze.
The day begins with jest and cheer,
With coffee brews and chuckles near!

The Winter's Breath Hangs Heavy

Whiskers frozen, a cat looks perplexed,
His tail is tangled, what's next?
Tumbling outside, he meets the snow,
An avalanche of fluff hits him, oh no!

A snowman's hat flies high with pride,
While ducks in the pond plan to slide.
The laughter rings through frosty air,
As snowflakes giggle, without a care.

A squirrel skitters, all clad in fuzz,
Chasing his acorn like it's a buzz.
But the ground is slick, his feet take flight,
He lands in a drift, what a sight!

As twilight wraps the day in white,
The stars come out to share their light.
With smiles and chuckles, we sit and sing,
Warm hearts dance while the cold winds fling!

Frigid Bloom of Memory

In the garden where frost bites,
Tulips wear ice like fancy tights.
Pansies chuckle in coats of white,
While daisies vanish out of sight.

Laughter echoes with snowflakes falling,
Squirrels with hats just keep on calling.
Old man winter's quite the tease,
Stealing warmth with every breeze.

Chasing mittens on a cold spree,
Hands tucked deep, oh where can they be?
Joking with icicles, what a sight,
Frosty giggles in the night.

Memories flit like birds in flight,
Warm cups, fuzzy socks feel just right.
In this chill, we find our cheer,
Funny moments, spreading here.

Shivering Serenity at Dusk

The sun dips low with pinky hues,
Snowmen dance in vibrant shoes.
Woolly hats bob and swirl with glee,
Chill whispers secrets, can't you see?

Hot cocoa spills, oh what a mess,
Marshmallows float, not less but yes!
Each sip brings giggles, a chocolaty grin,
As snowflakes pirouette, the fun begins.

Sleds fly down with reckless shouts,
Laughter echoes, what it's about.
Winter's chill, a comical plight,
As we huddle close, warm hearts ignite.

Dusk brings shadows, but not despair,
Mirth dances through the frosty air.
In each shiver, there's joy to find,
Memories made, forever entwined.

Shards of Light in Moonlit Shadows

Moonlight gleams on the icy ground,
Whispers of night in stillness found.
Snowflakes shimmer like pages of lore,
Each twist and turn, laughter galore.

Tracks of critters leave hints of fun,
Chasing shadows, all on the run.
Giggles erupt with each little slip,
Around the bends, see that wild trip.

Stars twinkle, a mischievous wink,
As icicles hang, don't you dare blink.
Games of tag in the frosty air,
Shattered dreams in laughter to share.

Woolly scarves wrapped tight around necks,
Comical falls lead to playful checks.
Moonlit nights bring a charming glance,
In chilly air, our souls dance.

Silence Wrapped in Snow

Soft blankets of white drape the town,
Whispers of winter, no frowns allowed.
Pillows of snow, a soft, chilly hug,
As laughter erupts from a cozy rug.

Pancakes flopped, oh what a sight,
Maple syrup drips with delight.
Each flip a story, told with grace,
In the frosty kitchen, laughter's embrace.

Mittens lost in the endless fluff,
Chasing the dog, oh, isn't this tough?
Each stumble brings giggles in waves,
While the snow gently covers our knaves.

Quiet settles like a deep, warm quilt,
With every chuckle, all worries wilt.
In this magic, so peaceful, sublime,
We find the joy, sweet, every time.

Frostbitten Memory of Sweet Slumber

Beneath the quilt, I dream of cheese,
A winter wonderland of melted ease.
My toes protest, they're cold as stone,
While visions of warm pizza float alone.

The alarm clock yells, a frozen beast,
I hit the snooze, let slumber feast.
My coffee's cold, my slippers lost,
Yet in this chill, I'm the boss at any cost.

The sun peeks in, a shy little glow,
While I pretend I'm still in the show.
The ice outside suggests a race,
But here in my bed, it's a cozy place.

Finally up, I greet the day,
With laughter brightening the gray ballet.
If frost had a sense of humor, you'd see,
It would laugh at my antics, quite joyfully.

The Quiet Song of an Icy Morning

Oh what a sight, the trees in white,
They look like my grandma sans her might.
The world outside, a frozen bliss,
Yet here I sip coffee, oh how I miss!

Birds in my yard, they hop and dance,
While I struggle to wear my warmest pants.
Frosty breath and a clumsy stride,
I trip on the mat, oh what a ride!

The ice on the window, a canvas of art,
Looks like my plans had a head start.
I giggle at squirrels, with acorns they scurry,
In this chilly maze, there's no need to hurry.

So on this day, let silly reign,
For laughter and warmth will break the chain.
With each chattering tooth and frozen grin,
I'll embrace the day, let the fun begin!

Echoes from the Depths of Hibernation

Buried deep in my fluffy nest,
My blanket's heavy, it knows me best.
I snooze with bears, a champion of rhyme,
Yet the phone keeps buzzing, oh what a crime!

Pajamas stuck like an awkward hug,
With dreams of sunshine and a mega mug.
Ice cubes tingling in my glass,
While I contemplate if I can pass.

Breakfast waits, a frosty tease,
But cereal's chilly; oh, my knees!
I laugh at the frost on my dog's nose,
We both prefer sleeping in cozy clothes.

The world outside, a crystalline maze,
While I snicker at winter's quirky ways.
In this frozen fun, I'll dance and sway,
For every chilly dawn brings laughter my way.

When Night Meets the Mildest Dawn

The stars waltzed out as the sun tiptoed,
I squint at the light, my brain's still slowed.
The moon yawns wide, a comfy sigh,
Saying farewell to the night sky spry.

My pillows chant from the soft abyss,
'One more hour!' I plead, that's my bliss.
Yet through the glass, the frost does beam,
It whispers, 'Get up! It's not just a dream!'

In pajamas thick as a winter coat,
I shuffle about on my toes, afloat.
Laughter echoes from my breath, a show,
Winter's clumsy ballet in the morn's glow.

So here I stand, a giggling fool,
Embracing the chill, I'll break every rule.
For even in ice, I'll find the cheer,
In silly antics, there's nothing to fear!

The Light That Cuts Through the Black

In the fridge, I found the light,
It flickered on and gave a fright.
Eggs stared back with frozen glee,
A breakfast dance, just them and me.

Coffee beans began to chatter,
As sugar cubes faced off in splatter.
A mirthful fight in the morning sun,
While socks still hide, I'm not yet done.

The toaster pops, and bread jumps high,
It lands on butter, oh me, oh my!
Jam's doing the cha-cha in a jar,
Guess breakfast is now a big rock star!

With crumbs like snowflakes on the floor,
I'm laughing hard, I'll clean no more.
A light that cuts, so bright and bold,
Turns my fridge into pure gold.

Echoing Shadows of the Past

Ghosts of toast in the morning glare,
Whisper of crumbs, a wafting air.
Yesterday's dinner fights my fate,
As I chase leftovers, oh what a plate!

The shadows dance near my chair,
Reflecting wishes, "Do we dare?"
Bananas plot in their hanging rack,
"Let's lure them in, there's no way back!"

The fridge door creaks like an old ghost,
It holds the secrets I need the most.
Pickles arguing in their brine,
Silly old fridge, are you out of line?

Echoes of laughter fill the air,
As I trip on socks without a care.
The shadows giggle, they love the show,
In this morning chaos, we've got the flow.

Crystalline Frights Beneath the Dawn

The sun peeks in with a drowsy yawn,
And icy chaos greets the dawn.
Frosty fingers slap my nose,
Like little gremlins, heaven knows!

The snowflakes flutter like angry bees,
Chasing after me with icy knees.
I trip on a path that sparkles bright,
A crystalline terror that gives a fright!

Old boots in a corner, full of gloom,
Wondering why they can't find room.
They grin and grumble as I go,
"Where's our adventure? Come on, let's flow!"

Behind the glass, the simpering sun,
Gently nudges, "Let's have some fun!"
I swear I saw a squirrel in white,
Waving hello with all its might!

Secrets Stirring Beneath the Snow

Under the drifts lies a rumbling story,
Of nuts and snacks seeking glory.
Squirrels unite, with tiny plans,
A fluffy army with wiggly hands.

The snowball fights with the winter sun,
Fighting its rays, oh what a run!
Each flake holds a chuckle, full of cheer,
As they sprinkle joy, and disappear.

Giggling secrets beneath the snow,
Of buried treasure, up they go!
Almonds shouting, "We're on a roll!"
While sugar plums dance in frosty shoal.

So when the dawn breaks and rises high,
Join the fun, give it a try!
For beneath the icy, chilly glow,
Lies laughter waiting to steal the show.

Dreams Adrift in Frozen Whispers

In pajamas thick, I trudge around,
Chasing warm cocoa, oh what a sound!
The cat's in the toaster, a sight so rare,
And I dodge the socks that float in the air.

Breakfast's a battle of jelly and bread,
With a toast that has danced right out of my head.
Slipping on ice, I slide like a pro,
While the neighbors all point, oh what a show!

The dog dons a scarf that's two sizes too wide,
He prances with pride, oh what a ride!
Muffins explode like popcorn in cheer,
As we laugh at the chaos, oh dear, oh dear!

But laughter ignites as the sun starts to wake,
With dreams of mischief in every pancake.
We'll feast on the folly of soft morning light,
As we revel in joy, all's well, all's bright!

Light Bending Through the Gossamer Ice

Waking at dawn, the blinds shaped like ice,
I squint at the sunlight, oh isn't it nice?
The dog's got my slippers, my feet start to freeze,
And I stumble like penguins, a sight to appease.

The fridge is a wonderland, food tamed and packed,
Who knew yesterday's dinner could just be snacked?
A pickle's a fish, oh what fun, yes indeed,
As I waddle around, in search of some feed.

Chasing the shadows, I trip on a shoe,
It's a booby trap left by the kids, oh so true!
I dance through the kitchen with breakfast in hand,
Like a circus parade, I made quite the stand.

And laughter, it sparkles, just like the frost,
In the land where the cookies and dreams are embossed.
With each little slip, I'll just take a bow,
For mornings like this, I wish them the best, somehow!

The Quiet Transition of Night to Day

As night whispers soft, my pillow's a sail,
I dream of adventures with donuts and ale.
Up with the sun, it's a race to get dressed,
But the socks are all missing, it's quite a jest!

The clock is a tyrant that ticks and it tocks,
While I stand in the shower in mismatched socks.
A toast jumps for joy like it's trying to fly,
Can toast have a vision? I wonder, oh my!

Coffee brews bold, like a knight in a cup,
While I balance my breakfast—a wobbly sup.
The cereal leaps, like it's ready to part,
On this fine morning, oh laughter's an art!

As the day takes its bow, I ponder and see,
How mornings are treasures just waiting for glee.
With hiccups and giggles, life rolls in the play,
transitions like this always brighten my day!

Fragments of Silver in a Dusky Realm

Under the covers, I burrow and dive,
With pillows for boats, oh how we survive!
Imaginary tacos dance on the wall,
Making my slumber a feast, oh what a ball!

Awake, I descend from the steep mountain quilt,
With dreams that were crafted from laughter and guilt.
My hair looks like icebergs, all tangled and wild,
As I greet the new morning, a sleepy-eyed child.

Scrambled eggs giggle on plates set for fun,
As I juggle my toast with some jam on the run.
The cat plays the piano, or so it seems clear,
While my coffee just chuckles, as morning comes near.

Fragments of joy in a dusky shell haze,
Where each moment's wrapped in a giggling blaze.
With laughter and dance, we all start to roam,
In this silly, bright world, we feel right at home!

The Aria of Snow-Cloaked Silence

The snowflakes dance like tiny fairies,
While I trip over my untied pair of my worries.
The world wrapped tight in a wintry hug,
Hot cocoa spills, oh what a smug mug!

Chirping birds now chirp from within,
While squirrels debate where to begin.
Snowmen stand guard with stick-like arms,
But I still worry about their icy charms.

The sidewalks creak with every clumsy step,
As I juggle my gloves, which I will misprep.
Watch as I slide like an ungraceful ballerina,
In this winter's show, I'm the funniest diva!

And though the sun peeks with a shy little grin,
I'm still slipping and sliding, let the fun begin!
Giggles echo under the frosty embrace,
In the arctic theater, it's all about the grace!

Twilight Dreams in an Icy Refuge

When dusk creeps in and the cold wind sighs,
I wrap my blanket and sense the world's ice surprise.
The chilly air boasts of mischief galore,
As I search for socks I know I once wore.

With each icy breath, I puff out some steam,
Speaking to penguins, they join in my dream.
The cats are plotting their frosty escape,
While we laugh at snowflakes wrongfully shaped.

The moon winks down in a glittery show,
As I stumble on paths both treacherous and slow.
But who needs a plan when laughter's the goal?
Let's dance with the owls and swerve out of control!

And in this great wonderland, spirits awake,
We giggle through snowflakes, all kinds of mistakes.
For nothing's as funny as nature's surprise,
In twilight's embrace, all worries will die!

Resonance of Heartbeats in the Cold

Hearts race faster than this morning's chill,
As I try to jog up that slippery hill.
Ice clings to my boots like a stubborn trick,
I'm just hoping I don't take a quick lick!

Chomp on some frost, it's the latest craze,
But I'd rather have pancakes, served with warm praise.
Snow seems to giggle as it tumbles and sways,
While I ponder the hours of tangled delays.

Snow fortresses rise, while I build a tall wall,
But as I lean in, I'm destined to fall.
The neighbors peek out, perhaps they will cheer,
But more likely to laugh — "That's the wintertime fear!"

Yet through all the stumbles, I wear a big smile,
Embracing the chaos, all cloaked in style.
For the fun is in laughing, come frost or come thaw,
Life's silly adventures, I proudly withdraw!

Shimmers of Hope Wrapped in Frost

In morning light glistens, the world shines anew,
Yet I feel so sleepy, oh what shall I do?
I'd seek out the warmth of my cozy old chair,
But the sun's got a plan — it'll melt all my hair!

Hot chocolate bubbles while marshmallows swim,
And I plot out my escape on a whimsical whim.
The icicles dangle like spears in a war,
While my dreams of summer are flung from the door.

The laughter of children cascades through the trees,
They dive into snowdrifts, with giggling ease.
And though winter clashes it plays such a part,
It wraps us in joy, lifting up every heart!

So here's to the cold and the fun it begets,
In shimmers of hope that no one forgets.
Life's such a hoot when the chill overrides,
Let's dance with the frost, on this wild winter ride!

Shivering Echoes from the Abyss

Chilly breezes tickle my toes,
I dance like a penguin, everyone knows.
The snowflakes giggle as they drop by,
While frosty breath rises like a cloud in the sky.

I hear a loud crunch, my foot slipped in ice,
I hope no one saw, oh isn't that nice?
The icicles laugh as they hang from the roof,
I just wish they'd stop telling the truth.

With snowball mischief my friends take aim,
My laughter is loud, we're all just the same.
As I wipe off the frost from my cheeks once more,
I wonder if hot chocolate is there in store!

The morning is bright with sparkly cheer,
But my nose is so cold, let me make that clear.
Yet within all the chill, we find our delight,
In shattering laughter through the long, frigid night.

A Dance with the Frozen Fog

In the thick mist, we stumble and sway,
Snowflakes fall, come out to play.
A ballet of shivers, we spin and we twirl,
As I trip over my own frozen curl!

With my scarf wrapped tight and my hat cocked askew,
I prepare for a tumble, yes, that's what I'll do!
A foggy ballet—very avant-garde,
But my moves aren't smooth; it's more like a shard!

"Watch out!" I cry, and we all burst with glee,
As I launch a snowball; it's a face full of me!
We giggle and squeal in this crazy chill dance,
Hoping the echoes of laughter enhance.

So here's to the fog and the prancing snow clumps,
To tumbles of joy, and our glorious bumps.
When the sun breaks through it turns into a joke,
As we recall our madness with each hearty poke!

Time Fractured Under Winter's Hand

The clock is confused in this wintery scene,
Time flies like snowflakes, crisp and serene.
Yet here I am, stuck in the freeze,
Where seconds tick by like a sneeze in the breeze.

I check my watch, it gives me a stare,
"Are you serious? Go buy some warmer wear!"
With each failing attempt to stay awake,
I look like a snowman that's ready to break!

I dance with the clocks while they laugh at my fate,
Spinning 'round time, it's a comical state.
My teeth chatter rhythm as I hop through the night,
"Is it time for cocoa or still late for fright?"

Under winter's spell, I muse and I muse,
Before I'm reformed into frozen good news.
In the depths of the chill, one thing is for sure,
Time's just a prankster I cannot bore!

Specters of the Morning Chill

Awoken at dawn by the specter's call,
I peek through the blinds, see frost on the wall.
"Did you just breathe!?!" A shadow exclaims,
As I giggle and slip, answering with names.

The spectral air whispers while I do a dance,
A snowman appears, led by his old pants.
He winks and he wobbles, so silly and bright,
As my breath forms shapes that take off in flight!

Oh, the ghosts of the chill bring a wink and a grin,
With frosty puns and jokes about where I've been.
"Don't slip on the ice, it's a ghostly mistake!"
Yet laughter erupts as the trees start to shake!

As the sun makes its way through the morning so bold,
We shiver and chuckle, defy the cold.
At last, we will find as that sun starts to rise,
That every chill ghost holds joy in disguise!

Remembrance Wrapped in Chilly Embrace

The sun's hiding, oh what a tease,
Pajamas crusted like frosted peas.
Coffee's brewing, smells like a hug,
But the spoon's stuck, don't pull too snug.

Laughter dances on the icy floors,
While the cat plots on the window sills' doors.
We trip on slippers, a silly ballet,
Who knew warming up could be so cliché?

Mittens juggling like hot potatoes,
But our noses are afeared, like frozen tomatoes.
In this chilly embrace, we'll stumble and cheer,
With every misstep, the warmth draws near.

As the ice melts in a glorious spree,
We'll dance in socks, a laugh-fueled jubilee.
From chilly vibes to warmth's sweet caress,
Who knew humor could be such a mess?

Frosty Tendrils of Fading Stars

Waking up to frost on the panes,
Last night's dreams linger, like funny trains.
The moon is giggling, still in its plight,
While I tell it selfies are not quite right.

The dawn breaks softly, like butter on bread,
A sneeze in the quiet, 'God bless!' I said.
Outer space chuckles at my sleepy face,
Frosty tendrils in a comical race.

Stars blink away, as if hiding their laughs,
While I trip on my thoughts like on wild giraffes.
Each twinkling joke, a punchline untold,
In the silence broken, laughter takes hold.

So here's to the twilight of giggles and cheer,
In the fridge of the cosmos, the humor's quite near.
As frost covers more than just rooftops and trees,
It blankets the world in whimsical freeze.

A Chorus of Dawn in Shattered Silence

In the morning light, an awkward rattle,
Coffee is playing its own little battle.
The toaster pops, like a sneeze in the room,
While we join in a chorus of morning's boom.

The shadows dance with a quirky sway,
As the fridge hums tunes in a jazzy array.
Eggs juggle in their carton-makeshift nest,
While my hair looks like a bird's crazy jest.

Windows frosted, voices scattered like leaves,
Tangled together like tangled-up sleeves.
Laughter erupts, in an unpredictable jig,
Where each slip and slide feels like a big gig.

So behold, the dawn with its comical grace,
In a shattered silence that picks up the pace.
With each news report, a peculiar spin,
Life's a funny tale, where we all fit in.

Marvels of the Chilled Canvas

Painting with frost on a canvas so bare,
I dip my brush in a frosty despair.
Winter's hand leaves a signature chill,
As I giggle at colors and awkward skill.

Each stroke is slippery, a hilarious feat,
With splashes of blue like cold fish to meet.
Shapes shift and tumble, like socks in a dryer,
As giggles bounce off, lifting spirits higher.

The sun peeks in, a mischievous grin,
While my masterpiece looks like it's wearing tin.
But who needs perfection when laughter's around?
In the battle of art, it's chuckles we've found.

So let's cherish the marvels of chilly delight,
As we paint our mornings with laughter in sight.
Even through mishaps, we create something grand,
In this frosted joy, we make life unplanned.

Sparkles of Stillness in the Air

In the quiet hush, snowflakes twirl,
Like ice cream sundaes in a frosty swirl.
Squirrels in sweaters, cheeks all puffed,
Chasing their tails, moments are tough.

Hot cocoa spills on a chilly sleeve,
While frosty noses make you believe.
That snowman grins, a carrot nose,
Is it just me, or does he doze?

The world's a canvas of white and gray,
Someone's doing flips – hey, that's not play!
Giggling kids on a slippery slide,
One bounces up, while the other hides.

With every step, crunch, crunch goes the sound,
Hoping my boots don't sink in the ground.
Laughter echoes, despite the cold,
Chasing winter's stories yet untold.

When Ice Kisses the Morning Sun

Morning light dances on frosty pines,
As icicles jingle like silly chimes.
A penguin waddles, trying to skate,
While a cat nearby plays the role of fate.

Mittens mismatched, a style so bold,
Laughing at how my fingers feel cold.
The sun peeks out, with a sneeze and a yawn,
"I swear I'm not melting," it says in a dawn.

Snowballs become all sorts of fun,
Launched at my face—oh, what a run!
Chasing my shadow, I trip, and I fall,
Wishing for grace, it's a laugh after all.

When ice meets warmth, it's quite the show,
Raining down laughter, with each flake's glow.
Stick out your tongue, catch winter's cheer,
As the sparkle of frost brings us near.

Dreams Entangled in Frosted Whispers

Night drapes around with a silvery sheet,
Blankets of twinkle make slumber sweet.
Snowmen gossip in the moonlight's gaze,
While hot cocoa dreams drift in a daze.

An owl hoots, giving a funny stare,
"Is that a snowball? Oh, I'm unaware!"
Trees whisper secrets to the stars so bright,
Crafting frosty tales of sheer delight.

Under the sky, my blanket's a sled,
I'll slide down laughter, right out of bed.
In winter's embrace, giggles arise,
With a frosty grin, I'll claim my prize.

I dance with shadows; I prance with the light,
Making snow angels feels oh so right.
As frosty whispers waltz through the night,
In dreams we find joy, taking flight.

Awakening Breezes of Morning's Kiss

A soft little breeze tickles my nose,
Waking me up in a chill that flows.
Frosted windows frame squeaky sights,
Of rabbits in slippers, oh, what a fright!

Outside the door, snow piles up high,
As ducks in boots take to the sky.
With honks and toots, they're playing a game,
With snowball fights, they're wrangling fame!

Tea kettle whistles, a song of my own,
Laughing at antics from creatures unknown.
Frosty fingers dance on my cup,
While giggles and warmth fill every sup.

So here's to mornings, oh what a thrill,
With laughter and joy, winter's unstill.
Grab your mittens, let's twirl and sway,
For chilly adventures await today!

Whispers of Winter's Breath

Snowflakes dance with silly glee,
Hiding in my cup of tea.
My nose is red, my toes are cold,
But winter jokes are pure as gold.

Puffing breath like dragon's fire,
Chasing snowballs, never tire.
Each step I take's a wobbly feat,
I might just trip on my own feet!

Squirrels giggle from the trees,
Plotting schemes with total ease.
They snatch my hat, it's all in fun,
I chase them down, oh what a run!

In scarves of colors, bright and bold,
We laugh at winter's biting cold.
So raise a mug, let's toast the chill,
To frosty morns that give a thrill!

Glacial Twilight's Lament

Icicles hanging in a row,
Swaying gently to and fro.
I slip on ice, it's quite a sight,
Gravity's not my friend tonight.

The moon winks down, with a grin,
As I wrestle with my chin.
Frosty fingers, one last fling,
I rethink this winter thing!

Penguins slide with style and grace,
While I tumble, oh what a race!
Snowmen chuckle, arms wide spread,
As I land bumping my head.

Stars above wink in delight,
At my dance beneath the night.
So let's embrace the snowy plight,
And laugh till dawn, what a sight!

Fractured Dreams Beneath Ice

In my dreams, I skate with flair,
Then I wake—oh, cold, beware!
Wrinkled blankets start to sway,
I lost my hat, it flew away!

The sun peeks in with a teasing grin,
While I struggle to find my chin.
Frosted windows are my view,
As I sip my lukewarm brew.

Hats get stuck on bushes low,
A sneaky squirrel puts on a show.
With every jump, I laugh and squeal,
Nature's antics, oh what a deal!

The world is white, a sheet of fun,
But cold toes vanish in the sun.
So here's to laughter, warm and bright,
In dreams that dance through the wintry night!

The Stillness Between Stars

In the cloak of night so vast,
Snowflakes shimmer, memories cast.
Laughter echoes, a silly sound,
As we frolic on frozen ground.

Mittens mismatched, what a sight,
Sipping cocoa, oh what a delight!
The chill grows bold with each new sip,
Toasty thoughts, let's take a trip!

Footprints lead in zigzag lines,
Chasing shadows, crossing signs.
We twirl and spin in silver glow,
With winter's whimsy, let it flow!

The world's a joke, wrapped in snow,
As stars above put on a show.
So let us cherish each frosty breath,
In the warmth of joy, defying death!

The Path of Twilight's Tender Glow

In pajamas thick, I stomp around,
The coffee pot's my battle ground.
With slippers on, I take a glance,
At all my dreams that sleep and prance.

The cat laughs at my sleepy ways,
As I stumble through the morning haze.
My hair's a mess, a wild bird's nest,
Yet still, I claim to be the best.

The toast pops up, it starts to dance,
Upon my plate, no second chance.
I juggle it like it's a hot cake,
And wonder why it starts to break.

The twilight's glow is now my guide,
As I sip my brew, a merry ride.
With laughter ringing, I chase the fun,
And greet the day, the battle won!

Heat of Memories

A photograph strikes, the memories flow,
Of summer days where laughter would grow.
In funny hats and mismatched shoes,
We danced like fools, ignoring the blues.

The barbecue smoke, a cloud of bliss,
A mishap waiting with every kiss.
As burgers sizzled, we flipped with flair,
Yet all we got was a sunburned layer.

In cooler days, we'd reminisce,
Of ice cream cones and that wild hiss.
"Don't eat it fast!" I'd hear them shout,
But sticky fingers were the way about.

Through silly stories, we bond and laugh,
Our hearts warm up with every gaffe.
With fondness now, we raise a cheer,
For heat of memories, so sweet and dear.

Cold of Reality

Awake to chill, the blanket hugs tight,
The world outside looks frosty and bright.
I pull my socks on, a mismatched pair,
Fashion faux pas? I just don't care.

The door creaks open, a breath of ice,
I step outside, and think twice.
The snowflakes swirl, like dancers in town,
Yet all I want is to be indoors, down.

I trip on the steps, a slip of grace,
Land in a heap; what a perfect face!
The neighbors chuckle, they know the score,
This morning dance? I've mastered encore.

With every slip, the laughter grows,
Reality bites, and everybody knows.
Yet through the cold, giggles ignite,
In a world where everything feels just right.

Voices of the Silent Morning Light

The morning light creeps in so sly,
Whispers laughter as it floats by.
In sleepy towns, the coffee brews,
And coffee beans play peekaboo blues.

With birds that chirp in cheeky tones,
They chirp out secrets, no time for phones.
While dogs in pajamas strut on by,
Who knew they could pull off such a style?

The sun peeks shyly, a playful tease,
Warm hugs of golden rays that please.
With every smile, the day ignites,
In voices soft that chase off nights.

So we laugh together, the world awakes,
The silent morning, a break from fakes.
In giggles shared and cheerful delight,
We savor life, oh, what a sight!

The Silent Intersection of Time

Tick tock the clock, what a funny rhyme,
At the intersection, we stall every time.
Lost in thoughts, we sway and weave,
As minutes pass, it's hard to believe.

Pigeons gossip as we wait for green,
While I tie my shoe—what a silly scene!
A honk from a car and I almost jump,
In this busy life, it's a bumpy lump.

With quirky hats and mismatched pairs,
We stand like statues without a care.
Time pauses here; it grins and winks,
At all our fumbles as the world blinks.

Yet slowly we move, with laughter in tow,
At the intersection, where time's in the flow.
Each moment cherished like a tasty treat,
In the funny dance, we feel complete.

Milton Keynes UK
Ingram Content Group UK Ltd.
UKHW021948151124
451186UK00007B/161